OBJECTIONS

TO

PUBLIC SCHOOLS CONSIDERED:

REMARKS AT THE ANNUAL MEETING OF THE TRUSTEES OF THE PEABODY EDUCATION FUND.

NEW YORK, OCT. 7, 1875.

BY BARNAS SEARS, D.D.

BOSTON:
PRESS OF JOHN WILSON AND SON.
1875.

At the Annual Meeting of the Trustees of the Peabody Education Fund, New York, Oct. 7, 1875, it was

Voted, That the Argument of the General Agent for Free Common Schools be published in the Proceedings of the Board, and also that such a number of copies of the same as he shall think proper shall be printed, under his direction, for general circulation.

OBJECTIONS

TO

PUBLIC SCHOOLS CONSIDERED.

REMARKS OF DR. SEARS ON SUBMITTING HIS ANNUAL REPORT.

You will have perceived that my Report the present year is compressed within narrow limits. I desired to present, in connection with it, a somewhat extended statement of the views I entertain, after the most careful and anxious consideration, on topics that have been forced upon my attention by those who call in question the utility and even the justice of any provision by the State for the education of the people.

Since our last meeting, the subject of public Free Schools has been more fully discussed in the Southern States than during any previous year. The protracted consideration of the Bill contemplating "mixed schools," by both houses of Congress, gave occasion to the opponents of popular education to rally their forces and make an assault upon the whole system. The defence by the State Superintendents and others has been equally earnest, and much more rational and convincing. No sensible and careful observer supposes for a moment that the Public Schools in any Southern State will be abolished. Too many of the people have seen the advantages arising from them, even in their incipient stages, to allow such a backward step to be taken. They perceive that the objections made are, for the most part, speculative, and often purely imaginary; while others, less decided in their opinions, think it premature to pass judgment on them before the experiment has been fairly tried. The main object of the opposition is clearly to avoid the payment of the school tax. All other considerations appear to be subsidiary to this.

The most general objection is, that the government has no right to tax the people for the education of their children. It is here implied that the government constitutes one party, and the people another, which, in republican States, is untrue, both in theory and in practice. It is also implied that the acknowledged power of taxation vested in the Legislature is so limited as to exclude the support of schools, whereas it is a discretionary power, which may, indeed, be abused, but for the abuse of which a remedy is at hand in the sovereignty of the people. Chief-Justice Marshall says, "The people of a State give to their government a right of taxing themselves and their property; they prescribe no limits to the exercise of this right, resting confidently on the interest of the Legislature, and the influence of the constituents over their representatives, to guard them against its abuse." A State Legislature has, therefore, a legal right to tax the people for schools. The question then turns on the point whether it has a moral right to exercise its constitutional power in this way. It has been maintained that the State has no such right, and roundly asserted that it is robbery to take the hard earnings of one man to educate the children of another. Abating the exaggeration of the statement, and putting it in the proper form, that the property of all is taxed for the education of the children of all, we would remind those who take this view that such was not the opinion of Jefferson, the founder of the school of political philosophy to which they profess to belong. He prepared a bill, to use his own language, "for elementary schools for all the children rich and poor." "One of the provisions of the bill," he says, "was that the expenses of these schools should be borne by the inhabitants of the county, — every one in proportion to his tax-rate." In another place he adds, "It is an axiom in my mind that our liberty can never be safe but in the hands of the people themselves, and that, too, of the people with a certain degree of instruction. This it is the business of the State to effect, and on a general plan."

The theory of our opponents is, that the government should limit itself almost exclusively to the protection of the rights of the citizens in their person and property. Their motto is, "That government is best which governs least." The fact is overlooked that modern society is far removed from primitive simplicity; that, as civilization advances, men are brought into closer relations with each other both individually and collectively; that, as they have more wants, so they must have more supplies in common; that, in these circumstances, they derive great advantages from organization and combined action, which were impracticable before; that the man who lived apart from others, and could bring his own bucket of water, and carry his own lantern, now, that he lives in a community where there is a division of labor public and private, finds it easier and cheaper to pay his tax for water and for gas-lights, and in many ways to employ others to do what he once performed with his own hands. The regulations of government must increase in number as social life becomes more complex. The more progress there is in civilization the more concert will there be in action. Public economy will come into greater prominence, and increased demands will be made on the government for the exercise of its powers. Excessive legislation on some subjects does not prove that there should be no legislation in respect to schools. It is only against needless or injurious legislation that we should be on our guard. For the above-named motto, therefore, we would substitute the following, as much nearer the truth and more accordant with reason: *Of those things which are necessary for the public good, the State should perform that and only that which it can do better than the individual, and leave to individuals that and only that which they can perform more advantageously than the State.*

That government cannot be pronounced unjust which takes nothing from the individual without public necessity on the one hand, and without rendering a proper equivalent on the other. And this necessity exists in every free government in regard to schools; and this compensation for taxes is made in the security and general welfare of society. It is a great advantage to a citizen to live in the peaceful enjoyment of all the means of individual, domestic, and social happiness and prosperity provided by an enlightened, provident, and well-ordered State; and for all this it is but just that he should bear his part of the public burden. Nor is it necessary, as is sometimes supposed, that every measure adopted by the State should be equally favorable to every individual. If one be less benefited than others by a certain legislative act, he will, in turn, be more benefited than they by some other act. Most laws operate with some degree of inequality. If, then, Public Schools are not directly of the same utility to all, and yet indirectly benefit all in a broader sense, there is no more injustice in taxing the people for their support than there is in doing the same for other kindred objects respecting which there is no dispute. The postal service, the improvement of harbors, the removal of obstructions to navigation from rivers; the construction of canals, roads, and bridges; humane and charitable institutions, and the public works of cities, and police regulations, — all favor some classes of citizens more than others; and yet no one pronounces the laws providing for them unjust. Perhaps no law passed "for promoting the public welfare" operates more equally for the good of all than that for educating the children of the State.

There are no such absolute rights of property as exempt citizens either legally or morally from reasonable taxation. The power of a State to tax is inherent and as universal as the power to govern. The only consideration that is left is, whether the necessities and interests of a State are such as to justify the exercise of this power in the establishment of schools. That question has been so often and so thoroughly argued elsewhere that it need not be discussed here, except incidentally as we proceed.

Another objection has been stated in the following words: "I object to this system, always and necessarily tending to uniformity, because it violates the law of nature, which is the law of God." But every human being has much in common with others, while he has some things peculiar to himself. Of what is individual and peculiar, some things are blemishes, others excellences. Now, to speak in the same manner and in the same spirit of things so diverse, is not very philosophical. What is common to all requires of the educator common treatment. What is faulty needs to be obliterated, as far as possible. Peculiar qualities which are good should have a normal development.

A child, so far as he is rational, participates in the universal reason. An appeal to this is, in its nature, the same in all persons, adapted only to their age and attainments. Every mind in a class made up of such pupils needs to be held to a common standard. It has been proved, by innumerable examples, that a boy educated in this way has more mental power and versatility than one trained by himself. Having a common interest with others, he is aroused by sympathy. The action of the class on his mind is as valuable to him as the instructions of his teacher. The faculty of reason has freer play and becomes more many-sided. His whole mental development is less abnormal, and injurious idiosyncrasies are thrown into the background, as they should be. Education in the direction of universal or abstract reason is like the centripetal force in the solar system; that in the direction of individual peculiarities is like the centrifugal force. The former tends to unity; the latter to separation and isolation. The best training of the mind is that which begins with the individual where it finds him, and from that point starts in the direction of absolute truth and reason. The individuality will always assert itself as a positive force, and the progress made towards absolute perfection will give the best possible development to a healthy individuality. Let me illustrate: There is but one Model Man for humanity, and all men are required to imitate him. The Scriptures give us no caution against imitating him too perfectly for fear of producing a "monotonous uniformity." The individuality will take care of itself. There will not only be variety enough, but it will be of the right kind; it will not be abnormal. The Apostle of Love and the Apostle of the Gentiles were more alike for being disciples of Christ; but they not only preserve their individuality, but they both have a far better individuality for their common discipleship. Thus the two factors, a different starting-point and a common goal, ever approximated but never reached, are both necessary to that variety which God designed. Such is the law both of Christianity and of nature. But we are concerned with this broad principle only so far as it applies to Public Schools.

First, as to the pupils. They are usually in school only six hours a day, for four or five months of the year, between the ages of about seven or eight and fifteen or sixteen, leaving a plenty of time for the development of their individuality. While in school, their normal individuality will be preserved; only faulty and repulsive peculiarities, blemishes, and weaknesses will be, as far as possible, weeded out. The different schools and grades of schools are under different teachers.

In the second place, uniformity in those simple elements of knowledge usually taught in the Common School is desirable. Let all the children resemble each other as much as possible in their knowledge of the powers of the letters of the alphabet and of numbers; of orthography and pronunciation; of the meaning of words and the grammatical structure of sentences; of penmanship, punctuation, and the use of capitals; of the fundamental rules of arithmetic, and of the elements of physical and political geography. Individual peculiarities on these points are altogether too prevalent.

If by "uniformity" is meant that the schools of all the cities and districts will naturally be taught and disciplined in the same way, nothing is farther from the truth. The School Laws do not prescribe modes of teaching and discipline. The County Superintendents and Trustees have little or nothing in common in supervising schools. They act independently, so far as they act at all on these points, — each following his own sense of propriety. The teachers, on whom the character of the school in these

2

respects depends, are entirely independent of each other, are no more "equal" than other persons. On one point, however, there is uniformity in the Public Schools: they must teach all the branches of an elementary English education, and each in due proportion, — which cannot be said of all Private Schools.

If the meaning be that in the same school and in the same classes there is a general uniformity, the remark is equally applicable to academies, colleges, professional schools, and universities. But how does this principle operate in fact? For more than half a century theological seminaries have sent out their classes annually, and yet no two clergymen so educated, though the instruction was uniform, have preached alike. The individuality of lawyers and physicians, who have been educated alike, is just as observable. If the objector had spent a part of his life in Prussia, or in those States of our own country where for a long period the people have been educated in the Public Schools, he would have known that individuality, except in its repulsive forms, in those who have passed through them, is just as marked as it is elsewhere. There is, indeed, some degree of uniformity in intelligence, civility, and capacity for business.

Thus we see what ground there is for the following assertion: "Now, the children of our State, in attendance upon the Public Schools, are daily subjected to this unnatural process, tending to absolute uniformity, to the obliteration of peculiar characteristics, and by necessity diminishing their capacity for happiness and usefulness. Upon the same Procrustean bed they must all be placed, lopped off when too long and stretched out when too short, that, if possible, the law of nature may be nullified and the order of God reversed."

Again, it is said: "The tendency of the system everywhere and always is to enforced attendance." "If the system is to be sustained by the compulsory exactions of law, it must also, as a logical necessity, be sustained by the compulsory attendance of pupils." "In all the German States, in Italy, in nine States in this Union, . . . compulsory attendance is the law." The author of this statement cannot have read the School Laws of those States of the Union to which he here refers. His whole argument is framed on the false supposition that nine States do now, and all States finally will, require all children to attend the Public Schools. Not one of these States requires a child to do so. It is not against Private Schools, but against ignorance and barbarism, that they (and we too) are making war. Nor is it true that the law, in any of them, lays hold of the child, and forces him to disobey his parents, dragging him to the Public School. On the contrary, it says nothing to the child, requires nothing of him, but lays its injunction on the parent, and requires him to give a minimum of education to his child, either in a public or private school, — enough to render it possible for him to become a safe and decent citizen.

In taking a speculative view of the logical necessity of the system, the writer appears as a closet theorist, and not as a practical man. In a complex matter, where there are many co-operating causes, he takes one line of thought, and leaves out all the rest; and, with this one thread of logic, talks of logical necessity, as if the practical man were to proceed invariably in the narrow groove of a single syllogism. What may be simple and easy in theory may be impossible or inexpedient in practice. The considerate man knows that to make a law is one thing, and to enforce it is quite another. There may be a logical necessity from a single point of view, and over against it many insurmountable obstacles from several practical points of view. Legislators are more swayed by the latter than by the former. Compulsory education, where it really exists, has, in its real aim, sole reference to the children of the ignorant and vicious. So far as I know, it is, in this country, enforced only in reference to them, and that, I believe, in only two or three cities. There is no motive to induce men to enforce such a law in regard to others, where the reasons of the law cease, but every motive to the contrary. Consequently such a law, even where it exists, never in practice affects the children of other parents. In fact, the compulsory law is not generally enforced at all. This writer is as sure as that the sun will rise to-morrow, that, if the school system continue to exist, compulsory attendance will be the law of the Commonwealth. Others, proceeding on the principle that laws which cannot be enforced in consequence of their unpopularity are as weak as tow, are just as certain that compulsory attendance can never prevail in this country. General expediency, not a syllogism, will decide the question. If there be such a law, it will not reach those parents who give any reasonable degree of education to their children, and it will do more good than harm to others who do not give their children any education. If there be no such law, we must deal with the ignorant as we always have done, relying on those moral agencies which have been employed by all the States from the beginning, and which are still the reliance of nearly all of them. The point now at issue is not that of compulsory attendance. We have nothing to do with that subject in these States. The true question now before the people is, "Shall we make a fair trial with our present system of education, or shall we abandon it out of regard to the objectionable features of another and different system?"

Reasoning from the monarchical States of Germany and Italy to the republican States of this country, in regard to compulsory attendance, is not very logical. The stringent authority of government is congenial to the sentiments and habits of the people in the one case, and uncongenial in the other. No inference, therefore, can be drawn from the practice of the former to that of the latter.

Assuming that compulsory attendance (which is by no means the same as the enforced education of neglected children) will be universal in these free States, the objector to Public Schools goes on to say: "Now compulsory attendance upsets the reciprocal relations and duties of parent and child, as God has defined and imposed them, and is, *ipso facto*, a negation of God's authority. By the system, the child is not in the hands of his parents, but of the State. He is to be taught such subjects as the State prescribes; his manners, his health, his politics, his morals, even his religion, are all subject to State control. The child belongs to society, and not to his parents." He then appeals to the Bible: "Honor thy father and mother;" "Children, obey your parents in all things;" "Ye, fathers, bring up your children in the nurture and admonition of the Lord." He adds, finally: "Shall the child, in obedience to his parents, as God requires, stay at home and violate the law? or, shall he go in obedience to the law, and disregard his parents, which God forbids?"

It is, no doubt, the Divine plan for parents to give

personally religious instruction and home discipline and training to their children; but it is not the Divine plan that parents should be their children's schoolmasters.

Teaching must be a business, a profession; and we are no more required to teach our own children in the studies of the schools than we are to make their shoes. Nor is it true that instruction given by others in spelling, reading, writing, arithmetic, geography, and grammar — the principal studies taught in the Public Schools — interferes, in any way, with parental duty or authority. The parent who sends his children to these schools can teach them what the Bible requires quite as well as the one who does not. Besides, fathers are the very men most likely to lead in all public measures for schools. There is no party in the State whose interests can induce them, or whose power could avail them, to force upon the collective body of parents a system of education against their will. The idea is wholly preposterous.

The law, in a few States, requires the parent to see that his children are, for a period of about twelve weeks in the year, instructed either in a public school or elsewhere. Parents, with comparatively few exceptions, thankfully accept the boon of Free Schools, and comply with the requirement. These are all the facts from which an attempt is made to prove that the child is forced to violate a law of God.

In regard to the principle so confidently laid down, viz., that the State cannot, in any thing, without impiety, abridge the parent's authority over the child, I would remark that there is another passage of Scripture which seems to have been forgotten: "Let every soul be subject unto the higher powers." Here both parent and child are required to be subject to the powers that be, because they are ordained of God. By Divine appointment, the authority of the civil government is superior to that of the parent. The will of the parent must, in the last resort, yield to the will of the government. The government is so important to society, to which the family is only preparatory and ancillary, that the family must be subject to its authority. The child belongs as much to society as to the family, and for a much longer period. He is protected by the government against the cruelty of the parent. If he violate a law, the parent cannot protect him by interposing his authority. If the State needs the military services of a youth of eighteen years, the parent cannot resist. If the small-pox prevails, and a city orders that all the children shall be vaccinated, the parent cannot say the child is under my control. If a ship in which he sails is put in quarantine, the father cannot command his son to come home. All this is as scriptural as it is rational.

In all civil matters, therefore, parental authority is limited by the exigencies or perils of the State. This law is as applicable to education as it is to any other subject. The question, then, is not whether the State can lawfully and scripturally interpose in the education of children, but whether its exigencies or perils are really so great as to demand and justify the interposition. To draw the line is, indeed, a delicate matter. But of the principle of State interposition, whenever it is expedient, neither Scripture, nor reason, nor analogy allows us to doubt.

It is said that, by the theory of Public Schools, "the State stands to the children *in loco parentis*." The Public School system rests on no such doctrine as that. No such principle is recognized in the School Laws.

The State stands in its own place, and leaves the parent in his. For its own sake, it aids the parent in training up his children to become good citizens, well knowing that, without such aid, a multitude of children will be neglected and become its worst enemies. This is the theory adopted by every State. It does not propose to bestow a bounty upon individuals, as such, nor to interfere with the liberty and just rights of the parent. Such complaints do not come from parents who have lived under this beneficent system, but from men who, without experience or observation, theorize in the closet on the subject. The people are beginning to see that they have a deep stake in this matter; that they are immensely benefited as well as the State; that by this means, and no other, can they educate every child without difficulty. When they have once enjoyed the blessing of Free Schools they almost universally open their eyes to all the great realities of the case, and give up their old prejudices. They regard these schools as their own, and glory in them as the "people's colleges." Are not Public Schools more controlled by the popular will than any others? Teachers are selected and schools controlled by those whom the legal voters, mostly parents, elect for this purpose. How is the teacher appointed in a Private School? Do forty or fifty parents individually make the contract, and does each one exercise his parental authority in settling the course of study, the text-books, and the rules of discipline? It is well known that the best Private Schools in the South are academies with preparatory departments; and that these are managed, not by the parents of the children, but by boards of trustees. Parents may patronize them or not; they can exercise no control over them. Other Private Schools are set up and governed by the principal according to his own ideas; and he, if he be a man, will suffer no dictation in his own chosen profession. The parent must put up with such a teacher as others approve. There is often no choice between this and going without a school, on account of the impracticability of maintaining two schools in the same place. Practically, the whole matter is managed by a few leaders, the people following; and it is just as safe to have those leaders regularly chosen by the people as to have them self-appointed. What has been so often said about individual parental control has no place in any respectable Private School; and is true only of family schools, which are now wholly out of date.

A still more definite ground of complaint is presented thus: "The Public School, in all its departments, is and must be utterly irresponsible to parents. This feature, though the system is on its good behavior yet with us, is already beginning to awaken, to some extent, the public attention to the mischievous tendencies of the scheme. The punitive measures of the Public School even now . . . frequently do violence to our sense of justice, and inflict irreparable injury upon the character of the child." "In many cases, despite the best efforts to prevent it, incompetent, corrupt, brutal teachers will be appointed. . . . Whatever subjects may be taught, whatever manners encouraged, whatever morals, whatever religion, inculcated, however aggrieved or wronged, we must be silent, acquiescent. For slight or imaginary offences, a coarse, vulgar teacher, vexed and goaded by cheap whiskey, may wreak his brutal wrath on your noble boy, your delicate, shrinking daughter." I quote this last passage with regret. Does the writer mean to affirm that the Public School system is less favorable to the appointment of competent and humane teachers than the system of Private Schools?

The State, when its system is complete, provides for the professional training of its teachers by means of Normal Schools, Teachers' Institutes, and by the visitation and instruction of Superintendents. Nothing has exerted a happier influence in improving the quality of instruction given than these several agencies. Every teacher is subjected to a careful examination by a properly qualified officer, before he can be lawfully appointed. Then a selection is made by another officer or Board of officers. Having entered upon his duties, he and his school are frequently visited and inspected, and compared with others, and if he prove unfit for his office he is dismissed. Can as much be said of the ordeal through which the private teacher is to pass?

It is precisely at this point of wholesome and firm, but humane discipline, that the Public School has greatly the advantage over the Private School for the mass of children. The interference of dictatorial parents is one of the causes of bitterest complaint with teachers generally. The teacher may be made the slave of a powerful patron, and the proper discipline of the whole school must yield to the dictates of one whom it is not safe to offend. The parent will believe the child (the most unreliable witness) and not the teacher, who is treated as a culprit; and there is no cool, disinterested party to settle the difficulty impartially. In the Public School, the parent goes directly to the Superintendent or other school officer, who is not only free from the excitement arising from being a party in the dispute, but directly and deeply interested in maintaining faultless discipline, both for his personal satisfaction and convenience and for the reputation of the schools, which depend wholly on popular favor. He hears the parent's complaint. He then goes to the teacher and endeavors to effect an amicable settlement. If he does not succeed, he next lays the matter before the School Board, and the case is investigated and settled. There cannot be greater security than this, both for the school and the parent. It is not the child, but the parent, who should seek redress. There is no part of the whole system of public education which is more universally satisfactory, where it is in vigorous and healthy operation, than its equitable and well-ordered method of school government.

The State employs its wisest and best men to provide good school-houses and furniture, qualified teachers, judicious courses of instruction, and just discipline; but leaves every citizen at liberty to send his children to Private Schools of his own choice. And yet, in view of these very facts, the objector says: "My soul sickens in the contemplation of the terrible condition to which we are hastening." And what is this terrible condition? It is that in which a State, for its own preservation and welfare, and for the general good, takes care that all the people possess the rudiments of knowledge by the only means which can secure that result. The author denies that the State, which exists for the purpose of protecting person and property, has the right to protect itself and its citizens against ignorance, lawlessness, and violence, by such a preventive as teaching the people. Thieves and plunderers are to be so far protected in their right to do wrong, that they can bring up their children to be like themselves; and the evil must not be touched by the State till it is past remedy, and is then to be visited with penalties. Little culprits are around our premises every day, with no occupation but pilfering; and yet it is not allowed to put them in school, and make useful citizens of them; but they are to be left to grow up, in swarms, as pests of society. In some places which are in just this condition good citizens are removing to other States; and how is this exodus to be arrested? By emigration societies? Public Schools will furnish a surer and better remedy. This is a practical question, and the sooner we meet it the better. If we deny the right of the State to protect itself in this way, the evil can never be removed. England has, from the time of the Heptarchy, tried the experiment of checking it by Private Schools at an expense that is perfectly enormous, and now confesses that it is a total failure; and is driven to the expedient of Public Schools by the appalling mass of ignorance that is growing upon its hands, and endangering the stability of the government. No other State on either side of the Atlantic will ever lavish so much money as England has lavished upon Private Schools. The experiment failing there, I see no chance for its success in any other country. Prussia, on the other hand, has educated her people as no other State has done; and the consequence is that, in proportion to its population, it is the most enlightened, influential, and powerful people on the globe. And yet universal education is vastly more necessary to a republic than to a monarchy. Free Schools have been longer maintained in republics than in monarchies. For more than two centuries have they existed in some of our own States; and no tax has been paid more cheerfully by them than the school tax. By no amount of argument could they be induced to cut off this right hand of their strength. The whole population think they receive untold blessings in the form of a prevalent public spirit, orderly and peaceable citizenship, general intelligence, enterprise, wealth, liberality, security of person and property, activity and energy in church and State, in comparison with which a school tax of a few dollars is as nothing. If the fears entertained by some are just, why have they not been realized in this long and wide-spread experience? Why does not some nation, State, or city, which has given it a fair trial, abandon the system?

The failure of Private Schools *for the elementary instruction of the people — for we are speaking of these only* — may be explained from their very genius, which is, in a multitude of important particulars, the very reverse of that of Public Schools. Private Schools are often established as a means of support, or for money-making, and conducted both with reference to education and to gain, in varying proportions. Public Schools are established and conducted with sole reference to the best and least expensive means of education. Private Schools are established, not in sufficient numbers nor where they are most needed, but where they will yield the greatest income. The teachers are self-appointed, for whose competency and fitness no one is responsible. They may be good; they may be adventurers; they may be objects of charity, kept in place out of mere pity. The teachers lay out their own courses of instruction, often with the most slender provision for elementary studies. There is no supervision of Private Schools. The teacher cannot grade his school. If he instructs by individuals instead of classes, he can give only a few minutes a day to each pupil. If he instruct, as he must, numerous small classes, where he attempts to classify all his pupils, he must hurry from one subject to another without time for plan or preparation. He cannot safely be firm and impartial in his discipline. He is liable to be in the power of influential patrons. Teachers cannot be distributed in numerous grades of schools on the principle of division of labor, each one being devoted exclusively to that for which he is best fitted. These, and a host of other disadvantages, lie not in any thing culpable in private teachers, but are inherent in the system as a means of general education. These schools exclude all systematic arrangement among themselves, by being wholly independent of each other and disconnected. We are ready to do all honor to individuals, societies, and churches by whose benevolent agency Private Schools have been provided for the destitute. Some of these are doing a work which will be held in grateful remembrance by succeeding generations. Private Schools of various kinds have their appropriate place among the means of education. But they are an unsafe reliance for the universal diffusion of knowledge, and lack the elements of economy and efficiency which characterize the Public Schools.

If we are to believe in the theory set forth in the various articles under review, it is well for the State to appropriate funds for the endowment and support of the highest institutions of learning for the education of the few, but not to appropriate one cent for those schools which offer elementary education for all the people. It is well for the State to encourage emigration societies and agents, but not Free Schools; though these attract, not the scum of European society, but families of wealth and culture. It is well for the public to tax itself for railroads, but not for schools, though the latter increase the population and the value of property as certainly as the former. It is well to pay enormously for a little doubtful legislation and a great deal of party strife and contention, but it is tyranny to go to the root of the evil, and, by such means as public instruction, to educate the people up to the point of giving their votes to none but competent and good men, and thus healing this running sore of the nation. It is well to pay high rates of tuition, which shall exclude the majority of children, perhaps, from the schools, in order to place our children, for a few hours of the day, where they shall not come in contact with the children of others; and yet monstrous for the public (which alone can do it) to educate, improve, and refine all the children in the streets and about our doors, so that contact with them (which in most cases is inevitable) shall endanger no child's morals or manners.

It is furthermore objected that "education would be, to the mere operatives certainly, a positive disqualification . . by arousing ambitions which must be for ever crushed;" that the progress of society would be retarded by universal education, because "civilization ceases without scavengers, boot-blacks," &c. To show that it is sin for such persons to better their conditions, the passage is quoted, "Let every man abide in the same calling wherein he is called." And, to make the matter still more sure, it is added, "God visits the iniquity of the fathers upon the children;" "The child, by God's appointment, inherits the physical, moral, and intellectual characteristics of its parents." The conclusion is, "Our modern fanaticism is wiser than God."

It is needless to comment upon these obvious perversions of Scripture; but it is natural to inquire what the people of Scotland, of Switzerland, of all the German States, and, we may add, nearly, if not quite, all the States of the Union, do for scavengers, boot-blacks, and operatives of every description, if the education of these classes unfits them for their occupation. We have observed but one effect in this regard, — the increase of their wages. The universal testimony of employers is that the value of service, even of the lowest grade, is in proportion to the intelligence of those employed. What a calamity it is for a human being to be shut out, not only from profitable employment, but from the light of the sacred Scriptures, and of all books, and for the soul that was made for knowledge and culture to remain almost a blank! How dreary the life, and how low the pleasures of one who can never taste the sweets of literature, nor know what is going on in the wide world, in this age of wonders, beyond the narrow limits of his own town or district! As surely as States come under Christian influence, and pursue an enlightened policy, the children of the degraded and dangerous classes will not be left to the sad inheritance of their fathers' ignorance, crime, and ignominy. The human heart revolts at the idea that men are not to be helped out of their wretchedness, even for the public good, on the ground that Providence would not have it so. The humanizing influences of the age, felt in every civilized State, come not, as is implied, from impiety, but from the divine precepts and example of the Great Teacher and Exemplar of religion and virtue.

Another paradoxical view is advanced. The argument that public intelligence is necessary to free institutions is pronounced to be "entirely unsatisfactory," and then we are informed that "there is a vast amount of cheap humbug about this matter of education," and that the education which a citizen needs is not given in the Public Schools. "The mere ability to read, write, and cipher, a smattering of geography and grammar, of history and science, is not education, and seldom prepares a boy for the intelligent and conscientious discharge of the duties of citizenship."

"The best school which human wit ever devised for political instruction was our old county court system, where the sovereigns every month, however untaught in books, learned from the lips of eloquent orators and statesmen the history and nature of their government, the aims and tactics of rival parties, and received the ablest instruction in the rights and duties of citizenship. In this way intelligent citizens were made, though they did not, and many of them could not, read the newspapers." I am afraid that, in the changes that have taken place, that race of politicians — great orators, statesmen, and patriots — have deserted the county courts, if they have not, like those times of ignorance, passed away. Besides, the question at issue is not whether one, while a boy, and while at school, or even when he is through with his school, is "fitted for civic offices," but whether his power to read and understand will, when he has exercised it in his manhood, place him in intelligence above his neighbor who has not this power?

Suppose some men are brighter without education than others are with it, how is the writer to make it out that the bright intellects are always with the illiterate, and the dull ones always with the educated classes? With the same capacities, and with the same opportunities for growth and development in practical and public life, will it be maintained that the educated boy has no advantages over the uneducated? If not, the argument is entirely sophistical. Knowledge and discipline are given in the schools; practical and political knowledge follows the schools, and comes of itself and with increased power in the advance to manhood and maturer years. The school gives the elements of power; life gives direction and development to that power.

Suppose the illiterate can learn many things by observation, by intercourse with better-informed men. Do they enjoy the monopoly of these opportunities? Can they observe better, reflect more, judge more accurately, and reason more logically than those who have at the start disciplined intellects, exercised memories, and minds stored with elementary principles, and with varied knowledge? Does an excursion in geography beyond the horizon of one's own home, and in history farther back than the days of one's grandfather, and a familiarity with the thoughts of the great English writers, and the enjoyment arising from the perusal of the daily, weekly, monthly, and quarterly press, unfit him for competition with those of his fellow-citizens who are destitute of all these things, and to whom the literature of the world is a blank?

If the argument against the necessity of "book learning" for the citizen is good, it is as applicable to private as to public schools. But who would be so mad as to propose that all these be closed, and the youth be suffered to grow up as ignorant as barbarians; and, in their ignorance, prejudice, and passion, to drink in the sentiments of corrupt party politicians, and to depend on such an education as a preparation for the duties of citizenship?

There are those who protest against the payment of taxes "for the education of the children of worthless vagabonds." They would set these *children* to work in clearing up the swamps that breed malaria. Such persons, of course, must think it cheaper, wiser, and better to leave them, under the sanction of Heaven and of just laws, in their hereditary condition of vice and misery than to educate them, though the contagion of which they complain spread like the leprosy, though theft and robbery and bloodshed and slaughter outgrow all legal restraints and remedial measures; though such of their number as are detected and punished only become worse and more desperate by incarceration; and, finally, though the "taxation wrung from an unwilling people" for detecting, trying, imprisoning, and supporting them in penitentiaries be much greater and more oppressive than would be necessary to educate them all in their youth, and save them and us from one of the greatest curses which now afflict society.

As to putting young children into the field at the age which the laws of nature have set apart for education, and thereby dooming them to perpetual ignorance, it is as preposterous as it would be to attempt to reap when we ought to sow. It is as impossible to reap in seed-time as it is absurd to sow in harvest-time. This is not the way to rid ourselves of "the brute tyranny of numbers." We cannot recall the right of suffrage, and yet that right will prove a curse unless its exercise be guided by intelligence. We must be for ever where we now are, or in a worse condition, unless we educate. Therefore, with Washington, Jefferson, and Madison, I say educate, educate, educate! There is no use in ignoring our perilous circumstances. Do not let the State refuse to save itself simply because in so doing it also improves, elevates, and saves individuals. To brand this as "Quixotic philanthropy" is easy, indeed; but it is no mark of wisdom.

I will close this discussion by indicating, in the briefest manner, a line of argument that is purely practical. It is well known that in all the Southern, and especially the Gulf States, good lands can be purchased for a moiety of their former value. This condition of property is, no doubt, produced by many causes. But men who have offered to sell their plantations even at a much lower rate in the far South, have given as the chief reason the insecurity of property in fences, fruits, produce in the field, and all the smaller stock of a farm, arising from the depredations of a low and ignorant population. The pilfering propensities of this class of people are, indeed, quite insufferable. Let good schools be planted in all these districts, and, in less than ten years, when the pupils shall have reached their maturity, the whole condition of things will be changed. Again, the system of slave labor being abolished, and that of free labor substituted, it becomes necessary to qualify men for their new condition by giving them intelligence enough to be their own masters. Freedom of itself does not make one an intelligent and useful citizen. This question of labor can never be properly adjusted with an ignorant people of blind impulses. They will sport with their liberty to their own injury and that of their employers. Nor is it for this class alone that Public Schools are necessary. Such are the improvements in the industrial arts, and such the competition in all branches of business in the same and in different sections of the country, that men who are far behind others in intelligence and skill will stand no equal chance with them. Agriculture is now the leading occupation of men in the South. That it is generally in a low condition, that only a part of the soil is under cultivation, and that not in the most economical way, is confessed by all. The more thorough cultivation of small tracts of land, a greater variety of crops, with a proper rotation, and a system of sub-soiling, manuring, and draining, would not only be more profitable, but would greatly improve the soil. But all this presupposes a more intelligent class of laborers. A still greater advantage would accrue from the introduction of manufactures. Raising only one or two kinds of crops, depending chiefly on bulky raw materials to be transported at the present high rates, and paying for their return in the form of manufactured articles, not only subjects men to all the risks of a bad season at home, or of reduced profits if the season is good abroad, but it burdens them with disproportionate expenses, and leaves them without the prosperity resulting from a multiplication of the branches of business which places producer and consumer side by side. Now we must either renounce all these essential means of prosperity, or we must educate the mass of the people up to that point of intelligence which will render the skilful practice of all the industrial arts possible. The Private Schools will never reach the great body of the laboring classes. They are limited, sporadic, and devoid of all organization and system. Contrast with them the Public Schools both in efficiency and in the scope, order, and economy of their operations. In the first place, there is a complete organization of school districts, school funds, and of school officers. All the parts of the State receive equal attention in proportion to their population. The whole working of the system is in the hands of men chosen from among all the people for their skill in the business of education. The highest educational talent of the State is placed at the head of the system. Others of similar character constitute the State Board of Education. The best assistants that can be obtained are sought for as county superintendents. The fittest men in each district are selected as local school officers. All these, each in his appropriate sphere, act in concert on the same general plan.

It is also to be remembered that the schools themselves are organized and duly graded. Teaching becomes a profession, with a system of promotions that secures permanency in the office. Normal Schools and Teachers' Institutes train persons for this special work. Thus the

system, as such, is complete in all its parts, and has the economical advantages which characterize all great and successful business enterprises, by means of combination, organization, and supervision.

This is the theory. We do not assert that the ideal is ever fully reached in practice. School officers and school men share in the infirmities common to all. Least of all do we maintain that a *new* system will, *at the beginning*, bring forth all its legitimate fruits. All that we assert — and the experience of more than thirty States bears us out in the assertion — is that, wherever sufficient time and opportunity have been given, the ideal has been reasonably approximated first in the cities, and next in the country.

www.ingramcontent.com/pod-product-compliance
Lightning Source LLC
LaVergne TN
LVHW011627120826
845150LV00012B/2361
9781418193607